PER*F*ECTION

It's Not What You Do

IT'S WHO YOU ARE

J. Wright Middleton

Copyright © 2015 by J. Wright Middleton

All rights reserved. In accordance with the U.S. Copyright Act of 1976, the scanning, uploading, and electronic sharing of any part of this book without the permission of the publisher constitute unlawful piracy and theft of the author's intellectual property. If you would like to use material from the book (other than for review purposes), prior written permission must be obtained by contacting the publisher. Thank you for your support of the author's rights.

Scriptures are from the Holy Bible, King James Version, and Message Bible. All Rights Reserved.

Vision Directives, LLC | www.visiondirectives.com

Contact author for bulk orders, speaking engagements, and book signings at: www.jwrightmiddleton.com

Wright Middleton, J
Perfection: It's not what you do; it's who you are / J. Wright Middleton—2nd Printing

ISBN 9798218028282

Printed in the United States | Third Printing June 2023

ALSO BY

J. Wright Middleton

BOOKS

Ice Cream Kiss:
A Mother's Drama Becomes A Daughter's Journey

Things I Wish He Knew

Things I Wish He Knew from Sons to Fathers

Dreamer, Wake Up!

Blue-Jays and Butterflies

****

STAGE PLAYS

Sunday Brunch Marriage Uncovered

The Magdalene Monologues

Like Mother, Like Daughter, Like Me

DEDICATION

This book is dedicated to every woman, man, boy, and every girl who needs to know they are loved exactly the way they are.

To my loving family, you all have been my teachers throughout this life's journey. I love you dearly.

To Joann, Beverly, Lakisha, Jason, Andre, Zina, Eugene, Elizabeth, and Mary Etta. To Darlene, Winslow and the Simmons family. God joined us together and I am grateful.

To Marlene. My Mother. To Nathaniel. My Father. I am a reflection of you both from beginning to end. Even in your absence, you are present.

CONTENTS

CHAPTER 1
Me Loving Me 1
   "Can I Say That?" 3

CHAPTER 2
I Smile Because 9
   "It's All Love" 11

CHAPTER 3
Humility 15
   "Only the Strong Survive" 17

CHAPTER 4
Light 21
   "You're It" 23

CHAPTER 5
Power, Presence & Femininity 33
   "They Have Enemies" 38

CHAPTER 6
Reflection 51
　"Is That Where It Came From?" 53
CHAPTER 7
Validation & Acceptance 59
　"Validation".. 61
EPILOGUE..**69**
BONUS CHAPTER.. **73**

"At a time in history when we feel alone and divided, Janelle reminds us that there is a greater truth keeping us from accepting ourselves and one another.

Honest and insightful, Perfection gives me hope—not in human things but in something greater than myself. This book was exactly what I needed to deepen my spiritual walk after living through unprecedented turmoil.

Perfection reminds us that God has a plan for us, we just need to recognize that we are perfect in Christ!"

Rev. Tracy Mooney
Senior Pastor, Asbury United Methodist Church

This is what started it all…

*Me loving me, helps you like what you see
you may not fully understand this clear identity
but trust me—this is the best me you'll ever see.*

*I smile because He loves me
I smile because He made me
And He and I both agree
that I'm the best me this world will ever see.
Clothed in humility, wrapped in a light that comes from within me and
with His company—I will walk the path of my destiny.
Yes, I am the best me you'll ever see.
Full of the power and the presence of His deity that's delivered through the
function of my femininity.
He thought it not robbery to become like me,
so certainly I must be the best me you'll ever see.*

*By His words, the world was framed
By His spirit, I was given my name.
I was existing before my existence, predestined
for now through His preeminence.*

*When I look in the mirror, I choose to salute the creation I see
not needing to be validated or positioned by man
I know who I am, and I like who I be,
Spiritual, Intellectual, Beautiful, and Free.
I accept me,
Yes, I am the best me this world will ever see!
That's my perfection.*

©2009 *Perfection*
J. Wright Middleton

INTRODUCTION

PerFection is a word used to suggest flawlessness and completely acceptable, and it is a word suggesting improvement not needed or the highest standard of presentation. It is a word that can fill us with great satisfaction or greater grief. But today, it is designed to help you see yourself through the eyes of clarity and truth.

Every one of us has had or will have a defining moment in life. It may be positive or negative, but nonetheless, it will be defining. It will be a moment that will force you to stop and watch your world move inside of you in slow motion. Just so you can get a panoramic view of what's really going on.

We've practiced being defined by every external circumstance we encounter, whether it's our shortcomings, abuses, or mistakes. We've internally diagnosed ourselves as unfixable yet put in overtime trying to prove to others that we're okay. We've exhausted our souls (mind, will, and emotions) with perfectionist activities and excellent appearances by painting perfect pictures with expensive oil-based paints—until we're all spent. And then the paint begins to chip away, throwing us into a panic, especially when it chips faster than we can retouch it or find the right filter for it.

It's as if all of a sudden, the thing that you have lived with and that has sat quietly in the corner starts to make noise, and it won't keep quiet any longer. Like when a baby cries, and you do all the things you normally do to keep it quiet, but it won't stop crying— Well, today, that crying baby is the spirit of God within you kicking up the dust. He's ready for you to be free. He's ready for you to be true, and He's getting you ready for Him, because ready or not, here He comes.

CHAPTER 1

Me Loving Me

"Me loving Me, helps you like what you see. You may not fully understand this clear identity, but I'm the best me this world will ever see."

At a time in my life when all hell was breaking loose in my marriage (again), I found myself at a loss of my inner identity. I was caught in a whirlwind of emotions that caused me to question what I held so solidly in place. I felt like I was thrown to the ground and broken into a million pieces, and I could see myself on the floor on my knees, trying to gather all the pieces, but I couldn't. I was shattered, and I had never been this shattered before. I couldn't pull it together. It felt like trying to put a sand puzzle together. It was impossible. I was internally unrecognizable to me.

It was during this time I was reminded of a dream I had. I was in a pottery room, sitting at the wheel making a vase. The vase was beautiful, but I thought there was a glitch on one side, a slight imperfection. So I said to myself, I'll just turn it around so no one will see the glitch. All of a sudden, giant hands came down from out of nowhere, picked up the vase I made and smashed it to the ground. It broke into a million pieces. I was devastated. But then I heard a man's voice say, "sit down and let me make the vase I want to make." I sat at the wheel and put my hands on the clay; he put his hands over mine and led me in the shaping. My hands were moving in the direction that his hands were moving. And even though my hands were on the clay, it was his hands shaping the clay.

In this season of breaking, the Lord began to tell me to write down everything I liked about myself. I had never done this before. I had never thought of it before. How could I even begin? The first thing I thought of was:

> I like the way I think.
> I like the way I process information.
> I like my mind.

You see, I'm a thinker. I prayed every day for years to have wisdom (because I felt void), and God gave it to me, but because I never stopped to look at myself through His eyes, I didn't recognize that I had it.

This process of listing what I liked about myself began to give me confidence. Not confidence in my qualities alone, but confidence because my Father was highlighting things about me that I didn't realize had value. I took my qualities for granted. Unbeknownst to me, at the time, He literally took me through the perfection poem line by line. He spoke the words to me, about me, and for me, so I could give them to you.

"CAN I SAY THAT?"

Repeat after me, "Me loving me helps you like what you see."
Say it again out loud,
"Me loving me helps you like what you see."

Does saying that sentence make you uncomfortable? How can anyone say, *"me loving me helps you like what you see,"* without it being perceived as arrogance?

A true sense of love starts with loving ourselves first. My favorite book, the Bible says, "Love your neighbor as you love yourself." The caveat of this statement is that pure, simple, uncomplicated self-love can really only derive from being loved by a pure unadulterated God. We are, by default, taught to love ourselves and others based on conditions that have been met or required standards that have been achieved. Through this lens, we are extremely hard on ourselves (and others) because we see ourselves from the inside out and then compare ourselves to something we consider to be more worthy, stronger, prettier, or smarter than us. By far, this is leaving us with a cave-like deficit that we try to fill or hide.

We've become more productive than our parents could ever dream of being. We are more educated, sophisticated, fashionable, talented, gifted, structured, sexual, and adamant in our attitude of non-conformity, which causes us to believe we are living in a superior form of freedom. Yet somehow, in all of the deals that we've done, when we go home at night and reflect on our day—replaying most of what we've said and done we end up feeling like we still could have done it better. So, we vow—tomorrow I will be fiercer, I will be stronger, and I will be sexier, bolder, louder, more in control, and smarter. Are you out of breath yet? Because I am, I have jumped on the hamster wheel with both feet and found myself on these pages.

Loving yourself has nothing to do with thinking that you are or trying to be better than someone else, nor does it mean exalting your value above the value of another. Loving yourself actually has nothing to do with anyone outside of you. It means accepting who you are, being confident about who you are, knowing your weaknesses, walking in your strengths, and choosing to agree with the God who created you.

Your life is a gift, and when you truly love yourself, based on the foundation of being given a gift, then you will be open to exploring and understanding the value, function, and uniqueness of that gift.

Every living person and thing is created for a reason—a purpose that resides inside of the being. Trees give oxygen and bring beauty to a landscape. They provide wood for fireplaces, paper for our use, and homes for birds. It's not a skill learned or taught. It's just for what they were naturally made. The same goes for you. You were created with a gift and a purpose in mind. And wherever you go, that skill and purpose go with you. You carry the seed inside. What is the thing that you do that comes naturally to you? You didn't go to school to learn it, you love doing it, and when you do it, you receive energy and give energy.

Loving yourself gives you the courage to identify your weaknesses and walk in your strengths. Being clear about your definite limitations will keep you from taking on undue pressures and allow you to enjoy the strengths of others. Instead of constantly comparing yourself to another, you become free to celebrate your peers without feeling like something is being taken away from you. Embracing this mindset will help you overcome insecurities as well as feelings of inadequacy.

Loving yourself is rooted and grounded in Genesis 1:27, being created in the image of God. *"So, God created man in His own image, in the image and likeness of God He created him; male and female He created them."*

The reading of that scripture should bring the next obvious questions:

>What is God like?
>What is God's image?
>How am I reflecting Him?

I know these questions can be subjective but let's just say that we all agree on its definitive, absolute meaning. The embracing and examination of these questions will send you on a journey of self-discovery through the nature of your creator. Once you embark on seeking out God's character, image, and reflection, you will then discover *your* image, character, and reflection. Upon that discovery, you should be equipped to identify and eradicate mindsets, behaviors, language, attitudes, and actions that do not reflect the nature in which you were created. *Disclaimer: we will not at any time display the full spectrum of God's nature and character, but we can, through submission to Him, display the best version of ourselves as we were created to do. This varies by individual. However, there are some common core characteristics from which I believe we all can benefit.*

If anger and animosity are behaviors you practice, these scriptures should prove to you that you are operating in a likeness that you were not created in, an image that is counterfeit to the true image of your creator, which is God, and God is love and the behaviors and attributes of love are:

>*Love never gives up. Love cares more for others than for self. Love doesn't want what it doesn't have. Love*

doesn't strut, doesn't have a swelled head, Doesn't force itself on others, isn't always "me-first," Doesn't fly off the handle, Doesn't keep score of the sins of others, Doesn't revel when others grovel, Love takes pleasure in the flowering of truth, Love puts up with anything, Love trusts God always, always looks for the best, Never looks back, But keeps going to the end. Love never dies.

This is the kind of love we need to generate from the inside and become the first beneficiaries of its action.

You can be the first partaker of this love. **You can** never give up on yourself. **You can** care for others. **You can** be content with what you have. **You can** be humble. **You can** be gentle. **You can** help others first. **You can** find better ways to handle disputes. **You can** forgive yourself and others. **You can** take a stand for what's right. **You can** have mercy on someone. **You can** trust God because He loves you and has a good plan for your life. **You can** love yourself enough to move beyond the disappointments and hurts of your past and let love continue to live in you by giving it out to others. **You can** give life. **You can** create.

The freedom of loving yourself empowers you to live beyond the limitations of another person's opinion about you. You are free not to give into teenage or adult peer pressure. You are free to walk the path that God has designed for you, which may not be conventional, but it will be very effective for you. Remember, you are created in the image and likeness of God.

When you fully accept who YOU are and begin to love the skin that you're in, the beauty inside of you will make everything around you just as beautiful. It will cause you to draw out the glory in others. You will be able to share the love you have and really be able to practice the verse, "love your neighbor as you love yourself." The way you see God will affect the way you see yourself. What is your view of God?

CHAPTER 2

I Smile Because

"I smile because He loves me, and I smile because He made me And He and I both agree that I'm the best me you'll ever see."

There was a time when I believed that my spirit was all God was concerned about. I believed that He loved me based on how I loved my husband. I know that sounds ridiculous, but when the only thing you understand about marriage is "submit" and you have no answers about what's not working, it's very easy to see how thoughts can become convoluted. Anyway…I felt like I couldn't get it right, and God was watching me suffer. I felt like I wasn't spiritual enough, and anything I wanted was of the flesh (sinful nature). It was horrible! I couldn't understand how to separate my spirit from my mind and soul. I couldn't understand why did God give me a mind, soul, and body if He couldn't use them?

One day driving down the road in a state of confusion, I heard Him say, "I love all of you, mind, body, and soul. I created you a tri-part being." I almost ran the car off the road. God loved all of me! He created all of me! He gave me everything I needed to function in every environment He created. A light bulb had been turned on, and I got it. At first, I couldn't fathom that God loved all of me. All of me; even the parts that I thought weren't so lovable? Yes. Even those parts.

"IT'S ALL LOVE"

There is a certain joy and security that comes with knowing you are loved. Do you remember the words to an old song, *"this joy that I have, the world didn't give it to me, and the world can't take it away?"* When you know that your existence is solely based on a love that never changes, it will bring a smile to your face that begins on the inside; a smile that has nothing to do with your external conditions. It's a smile that lasts and stands regardless of the obstacles you face. It's a smile that reminds you—you are not your environment, your trials, your failures, or your struggles. Despite what you have been through you have what you need to rise above every circumstance. God's love for you is so intense that He'd never leave you without what you need to survive and thrive. Will unfavorable events arise? Yes. But you are equipped with God's wisdom and tenacity to find your way through them all. Remember James 1v. 2-3; *Consider it nothing but joy whenever you fall into various trials knowing that your faith is being tested so that you will learn how to endure. And through that endurance you will perfectly mature and completely develop. And if you need wisdom do not hesitate to ask God for it with the assurance that He will give it to you; because He gives it to those that ask.*

You are and will always be a child of God, and if He thought you were worth being here, then agree with Him and smile!

You are a one-of-a-kind make and model. Complete with your own personal VIN and license plate. God put thought into creating you and placing you in the world. God never overlooks any of the details of His children, and he paid great attention to you, down to the last element—even numbering the hairs on your head. (Luke 12 v.7) God told Jeremiah; I knew you before you were formed in your mother's womb. That means He knew everything that Jeremiah would and would not do. He planned Jeremiah's birth, death, and everything in between. He knew Jeremiah's sins before he committed them, and He still ordained Jeremiah as a prophet and gave him an everlasting name.

God's love and creative design of you was based on His goodness and your purpose. He knows you! Think about this – you are very aware of your thoughts, feelings and secret actions – so is God and He still loves you deeply. He does not disqualify you or count your mistakes.

Psalm 139 The Message Bible

"You know when I leave and when I get back; I'm never out of your sight. You know everything I'm going to say before I start the first sentence. I look behind me, and you're there, then up ahead, and you're there, too—your reassuring presence, coming and going. (v. 2-5)

Oh yes, you shaped me first inside, then out; you formed me in my mother's womb. I thank you, High God—you're breathtaking! Body and soul, I am marvelously made! I worship in adoration—what a creation! You know me inside and out; you know every bone in my body; You know exactly how I was made, bit by bit, how I was sculpted from nothing into something. Like an open book, you watched me grow from conception to birth; all the stages of my life were spread out before you, the days of my life all prepared before I'd even lived one day." (v.13-16)

PERFECTION

God's acceptance and approval of you are NOT based on anything you do. It's all based on the fact that He has decided to love you. He has decided to make sure you and I have the opportunity to spend eternity with Him, and He has decided not to wait for us to get it right but to help us get it right through His son Jesus Christ. This should put a smile on your face.

There are no "dirty little secrets" that you can hide that would keep God from loving you. He's already made His decision, and this should empower you to get up each morning with an internal glow knowing that God is smiling on you. Every morning He gives you the opportunity to show the world how grand you are because you are here. He just loves you so He could show you off to the world as an example of His creativity, His mind, and His love.

God is waiting for you because He needs your expression of Him on the earth. You have been given a unique way to convey His beauty, His love, His messages, and His thoughts. He is a God of variety and if you doubt it, just look at the variation of colors, flowers, trees, birds, animals, and fish, and also look at yourself. Embrace what you see because your creator is embracing you.

Right now, think on the position you have given God in your life and ask yourself, if you have accepted His love for you, because without accepting His love you will continue to look for someone to love the doubt away, and no one can fill a hole like that.

Internal love melts anger, fear, and unforgiveness away. No one can love you strong enough to make you love yourself. You are holding yourself hostage to a mistake that has already been forgiven. You are bitter toward yourself because you feel like you should have known better, wondering why you didn't leave sooner, asking how could you have let this happen?! Running yourself into the ground with negative and accusatory self-talk but God is asking you to let it go and let His love heal you. Let it uproot the bitterness. His love comes in like a flashlight looking for those dark, hidden places that you've locked away. His love reveals to you what's causing you harm and what you need to let go of. His love highlights the beauty inside of you that others need to experience. And His love is what loved us first. His love is redemptive.

> *Redemptive Love is a love that calls out to you and into you for the betterment of yourself.*
>
> *Redemptive Love*
>
> *The love that brings life to life through a personal death. The love that nurtures forgiveness of the unspeakable and restoration to the lost.*
>
> *I once was lost, but now I'm found*
> *By the river of forgiveness, drinking in its sweet waters of love and redemption.*
>
> *Redemptive Love is scoffed at, mocked, and misinterpreted due to its selflessness*
>
> *But the heart it caresses and the spirit it revives is forever grateful.*

PERFECTION

And although at times it makes attempts to re-ransom itself, it always learns that the love, the

Redemptive Love that found it dead—died so it

could live perfect.

Its value is Priceless, Infinite, Eternal, and Unable to be improved, Complete, and Secure.

Redemptive Love offers love not in spite of but because of unlovableness.

See, I smile because God loves me, and that gives me the power to wake up and keep smiling.

CHAPTER
3

Humility

PERFECTION

"Clothed in humility wrapped in a light that comes from within me & with His company, I will walk the path of my destiny."

Throughout the ten thousand lessons that I've learned thus far, I was enlightened by God that I had an "unteachable spirit." Needless to say, I was once again shocked, because I thought I was an excellent learner. However, I found out that I was a horrible student. I was horrible because I was my own teacher. I was the teacher and the student. This meant I had complete control over what I learned and how I learned. I learned in my way, at my pace, and I chose the subjects that were of interest to me, which were usually chosen based on the least amount of pain and discomfort they produced. Experience is the best teacher, we say and to a degree that's true in a sense. Experience is a good teacher, but it's not the best teacher and definitely not the only teacher. The Holy Spirit is the ultimate teacher, and his teaching leads you and guides you into all truth. The truth about any area you want or need to learn about, especially God.

Now in order to be taught by Him, I had to realize and admit that I didn't know everything. Scary, I know, but I did it. I had to relinquish what I believed and what I held as pillars in my life and let God teach me the truth. If experience were to be my teacher than my knowledge would be limited to what only I experienced. The purpose of that saying assumes that we garner life lessons from our experiences. But not everyone takes the time to stop and look at their experiences through a learning lesson lens. In walks the Holy Spirit. Let Him transform my thinking and my way of doing things. I had to stop letting experience be my teacher because it had become my bible. That which you learn has influence over the formation of your thoughts and beliefs.

"ONLY THE STRONG SURVIVE"

Humility has been described as strength under control. Listen to the phrase, "Strength under control." The natural response to strength is never to control it. There is an ordinate satisfaction in being able to demonstrate prowess in any form. In education, we strive to be scholarly, in beauty, we strive to be flawless, in fashion, we strive to be trend-setters, in finances, we strive to be among the elite and in society we want to be an influencer. In these examples, striving could very well land you where you want to be, but when you arrive, will you be able to allow your arrival not to define you and snub those still in the strive?

True humility is demonstrated when you are able to show deference toward someone else over yourself. When you know that your strengths do not make you better, but they have laden you with the responsibility to make way for someone else. Your shoulders have now become strong enough to let someone else stand on them.

Let's not confuse the word humility with humiliation. Although the roots of these words are the same and have the same meaning, their expression is totally different. Humility is to bring oneself down low, not as in sorrow but as in preference. Humiliation is to be brought down low by no participatory action of your own but by force because of a lofty mindset. Remember, love is not puffed up. Humility is a choice. Humiliation is by force.

PERFECTION

> ❖ *1 Peter 5; 5-6 "clothes yourselves with humility (and be free from pride and arrogance) toward one another. For God sets Himself against the proud (and He opposes, frustrates, and defeats them), but to the humble, He gives grace. Therefore, humble YOURSELVES under the mighty hand of God, that in due time He will exalt you.*

Humility is something you do of your own free will. If you know that God has created every person on the earth, along with yourself, then you should be able to see others and love others as you love yourself.

There are no earthly possessions or positions that make your life more valuable than someone else's. You are God's creation, and so is the person that's getting on your last nerve…LOL!

The lack of humility, which is pride, has everything to do with how you think of yourself in comparison to someone else. Whenever you put something or someone down in order to lift yourself or your perceived image higher, you are not acting in humility. It's absolutely one hundred percent pride.

Jesus, who was God's flesh son, became like one of us and did not think anything of it. The teacher became the student, fully embodying all of our issues so that we could have the opportunity to connect with our Heavenly Father. He did this knowing that we could very well decide not to take the opportunity that He suffered to give us.

For any of us to ever think that we are a greater creation than any other God-created human being is total self-deception.

The sacrifice of Jesus Christ has leveled the playing field. Christ died for the rich and the poor, the intellectual and the illiterate, the blind and the seeing, the weak and the strong, the pastor and the laymen. It is men who classify and categorize. In Christ, there are two categories—the sinner—and the sinner who has been saved from the penalty of his sin.

> ***Galatians 6 v.3amp***—*"If any person thinks himself somebody (too important to condescend and shoulder another's load) when he is nobody (of superiority except in his own estimation), he deceives and deludes and cheats himself."*

To humble yourself is a choice. An act of your will all on its own. It's a posture of your heart and a condition of your mind. You, being willing to submit yourself to the notion of another way, or the preference of another, or another's proven wisdom. It in no way diminishes your power but actually merges your power with the wisdom to identify that you may not know.

One Sunday morning I was in the mirror getting dressed for church and Holy Spirit said, "Humble yourself before me". I was shocked to hear it but immediately recognized that in my heart I was gloating on my look and the self presentation that I was going to make in church. Immediately I paused and apologized. I felt so ridiculous but I knew what was meant by what I heard. I started looking in my closet for the dreariest, muted outfit I could find and then He told me to put on my cream pantsuit. Now I'm confused because the pantsuit was not fancy but the color itself stood out. That's when I got my lesson. The humility He asked for wasn't about what I wore but it was about the posture and the focus of my heart. At that time, my focus was getting dressed t impress while going to the place we gather to honor God was not my focus. Today it would be equivalent to posting something spiritual on social media to see hao many likes it gets. It's accepting who you are in and through the light of God's word. No more, no less.

The Holy Spirit who leads you and guides you into all truth and shows you things to come will be your leader. In this posture, His light will gleam through your life and illuminate the gift that He made you to be. That internal light will be the guide that leads you to your destiny.

Here is a quote I read and liked:

"Humility has nothing to do with depreciating ourselves and our gifts in ways we know to be untrue. Even "humble" attitudes can be masks of pride. Humility is that freedom from ourselves that enables us to be in positions in which we have neither recognition nor importance, neither power nor visibility, and even experience deprivation, and yet have joy and delight. It is the freedom of knowing that we are not in the center of the universe, not even in the center of our private universe."

—David F. Wells, *Losing Our Virtue*

Humbling ourselves to God means allowing His instruction to guide every part of our lives, even down to the clothes we wear; trusting that He will not make us ashamed and He will lift you up. ***James 4:10*** *"Humble yourselves before the Lord and He will lift you up in honor."*

CHAPTER 4

Light

"Wrapped in a light that comes from within me. And with His company, I will walk the path of my destiny."

Destiny. It has such a big far away sound. Or is it just me? Destiny sounds like I'll get there one day after a long while, and I hope I don't miss it. Because destiny is a futuristic landing spot that my present actions will settle me in—I choose to look at destiny as my destination. I asked the Lord (I do this a lot. It's the only way I can live), about destiny and why that word left me in limbo. He said, how do you know you've landed where you are supposed to be if you've never been there before? Then He showed me where I was going and where I was supposed to be. This book is a destiny because I was told this was the next book, He wanted me to write. How do you know when you get to destiny or your destination? You will see it before you get there.

Needless to say, I've written 2 books since then and didn't have any direction for them. They are good books but were not in line with destiny timing. The excitement, vision, provision, and surge of energy around this book are signals to me that the light within me is in agreeance.

It is the leading of the Holy Spirit that will walk you on the path of destiny. Destiny isn't mysterious, it's just seen by a different pair of eyes, and it takes the light of the Holy Spirit to lead the way.

"YOU'RE IT"

Where there is darkness, the light must shine to cast the darkness aside. If your darkness is light, then how great is the darkness that dwells inside?

The statement above sounds like a riddle, but it's not. You are a light that should be set on a hill so that men (people) will see your good works and glorify your Father in heaven.

The brightest thing seen in you should come from within you. Which leads to the question, what is truly inside of you?

Perfection is not what you do; it's who you are. You have the right to express the person that God created you to be the confidence to display that person unapologetically and the wisdom to know that person is who he or she is because of God's plan and sovereignty. If I say it in any other way, you may be inclined to think it's about your performance, and in sober, honestly, no one has a perfect life performance. No one person is humanly capable of living a perfect life based on actions.

It's the mistakes, down times, hard places, and lessons learned that give us insight and navigational skills throughout life. In other words, it's the experience of ugly imperfections that are the foundation of the surety and depth of our statements and actions.

It is not God's will for man to present an image devoid of human frailty and the need for His majesty. However, it is the will of man's pride to present such an image that shows no need for God's intervention or absolute surroundings. We are a flesh and blood creation subject to the failures of poor decision-making and the uncertainty of our natural environment, the elements of the earth. This does not mean that our lives are indeed headed only for doom and gloom, but it does mean due to the potential of being apt to make mistakes, have regrets, and experience pain, that we are not in and of ourselves or by the way of actions, perfect.

Again, perfection can by no means be achieved by what we do. It must be unequivocally accepted as a gift from God through the acceptance of the death of His son Jesus Christ and the resurrection power we have in Him.

What does your perfection look like?
If you ever find yourself suffering or battling with:

- ❖ Low self-esteem
- ❖ Insecurity
- ❖ Feelings of inadequacy
- ❖ Performance anxiety
- ❖ Self-comparison (comparing yourself with others)
- ❖ Fear of rejection
- ❖ Fear of not being good enough or feeling like you're not good enough
- ❖ Trying to fit into someone else's vision
- ❖ Looking for acceptance
- ❖ Keeping old wounds fresh and looking for people to heal them
- ❖ Keeping quiet when you should speak up
- ❖ Trying to live beneath the radar
- ❖ Agreed with something you shouldn't have
- ❖ Subjecting yourself to physical, mental, or emotional abuse

PERFECTION

- ❖ If you're waiting for someone to release you in the plan of God for your life
- ❖ If you believe you cannot move forward until someone else moves
- ❖ If you are allowing past mistakes to stop you from doing what's on your heart.

Then you need to hear that

YOU ARE PERFECT, AND YOUR PERFECTION IS IN CHRIST!

Let me be clear that perfection has nothing to do with what you do or your performance. It's all about what Christ did for you, which makes you who you are. So, the question remains,

"If I'm *perfect*, how do *I* deal with *my* stuff"?

The Solution Is Life on God's Terms
(Romans 8 MSG)

With the arrival of Jesus, the Messiah, that fateful dilemma is resolved. Those who enter into Christ's being here for us no longer have to live under a continuous, low-lying black cloud. A new power is in operation. The Spirit of life in Christ, like a strong wind, has magnificently cleared the air, freeing you from a fated lifetime of brutal tyranny at the hands of sin and death.

God went for the jugular when he sent his own Son. He didn't deal with the problem as something remote and unimportant. In his Son, Jesus, he personally took on the human condition and entered the disordered mess of struggling humanity in order to set it right once and for all. The law code was weakened as it always was by fractured human nature; it could never have done that.

The law always ended up being used as a Band-Aid on sin instead of a deep healing of it. And now, what the law code asked for but we couldn't deliver is accomplished as we simply embrace what the Spirit is doing in us instead of redoubling our efforts.

Those who think they can do it on their own end up obsessed with measuring their own moral muscle but never get around to exercising them in real life.

▶ Without this clarity, what we end up producing and perfecting are behavior modifications. We tweak our actions and words to become spiritually politically correct, but we never deal with the heart issues, the root issues, the truth. So we become frustrated with God and His word, opening the door for the enemy to tell us—it doesn't work.

Those who trust God's action in them find that God's Spirit is in them—living and breathing

PERFECTION

God! Obsession with self in these matters is a dead end; attention to God leads us out into the open, into a spacious, free life.

Focusing on the self is the opposite of focusing on God. Anyone completely absorbed in self ignores God and ends up thinking more about self than God. That person ignores who God is and what he is doing, and God isn't pleased with being ignored.

- Go back to the list and mention how all of those things are about us.

Anyone, of course, who has not welcomed this invisible but clearly present God, the Spirit of Christ, won't know what we're talking about. But for you who welcome him, in whom he dwells—even though you still experience all the limitations of sin—you yourself experience life on God's terms. But if God himself has taken up residence in your life, you can hardly be thinking more of yourself than of him.

- I may have pain, but by His stripes, I am healed.
- I may not have the answer right this second, but Christ has been made wisdom to me, and God gives wisdom to every man that asks.
- Great is the peace of my children, and they will be taught of the Lord.

► I've believed for a long time, but God is a rewarder of them that diligently seek Him. I will not throw my confidence away—my hope is in the Lord, the Maker of Heaven and earth.

It stands to reason, doesn't it, that if the alive-and-present God who raised Jesus from the dead moves into your life, he'll do the same thing in you that he did in Jesus, bringing you alive to himself? When God lives and breathes in you (and he does, as surely as he did in Jesus), you are delivered from that dead life. With his Spirit living in you, your body will be as alive as Christ's!

So don't you see that we don't owe this old do-it-yourself life one red cent. There's nothing in it for us, nothing at all. There are things to do and places to go! The best thing to do is give it a decent burial and get on with your new life; God's Spirit beckons.

This resurrection life you received from God is not a timid, grave-tending life. It's adventurously expectant, greeting God with a childlike "What's next, Papa?" God's Spirit touches our spirits and confirms who we really are. We know who he is, and we know who we are: Father and children. And we know we are going to get what's coming to us— an unbelievable inheritance! We go through exactly what Christ goes through. If we go through the hard

times with him, then we're certainly going to go through the good times with him!
        —Romans chapter 8 The Message Bible

- I AM PERFECT, AND MY PERFECTION IS IN CHRIST!

What God has given you, (the gifts that He has given you), the way He created you, functions perfectly for what He has for you to do! You are perfect for the vision God has for you! Your light and purpose should never be held in someone else's light.

2 Corinthians 10: 12-15 AMP

> *12Not that we [have the audacity to] venture to class or [even to] compare ourselves with some who exalt and furnish testimonials for themselves! However, when they measure themselves with themselves and compare themselves with one another, they are without understanding and behave unwisely.*
> *13We, on the other hand, will not boast beyond our legitimate province and proper limit, but will keep within the limits [of our commission which] God has allotted us as our measuring line and which reaches and includes even you.*
> *14For we are not overstepping the limits of our province and stretching beyond our ability to reach, as though we reached not (had no legitimate mis-*

> *sion) to you, for we were [the very first] to come even as far as to you with the good news (the Gospel) of Christ.*
>
> *[15]We do not boast, therefore, beyond our proper limit, over other men's labors, but we have the hope and confident expectation that as your faith continues to grow, our field among you may be greatly enlarged, still within the limits of our commission.*

What you say about yourself means nothing in God's work. It's what God says about you that makes the difference!

Ephesians 1

> *[2]May grace (God's unmerited favor) and spiritual peace [which means peace with God and harmony, unity, and undisturbedness] be yours from God our Father and from the Lord Jesus Christ.*
>
> *[3]May blessing (praise, laudation, and eulogy) be to the God and Father of our Lord Jesus Christ (the Messiah), Who has blessed us in Christ with every spiritual (given by the Holy Spirit) blessing in the heavenly realm!*
>
> *[4]Even as [in His love] He chose us [actually picked us out for Himself as His own] in Christ before the foundation of the world, that we should be holy (consecrated and set apart for Him) and*

blameless in His sight, even above reproach, before Him in love.

⁵For He foreordained us (destined us, planned in love for us) to be adopted (revealed) as His own children through Jesus Christ, in accordance with the purpose of His will [[b]because it pleased Him and was His kind intent]—

⁶[So that we might be] to the praise and the commendation of His glorious grace (favor and mercy), which He so freely bestowed on us in the Beloved.

⁷In Him we have redemption (deliverance and salvation) through His blood, the remission (forgiveness) of our offenses (shortcomings and trespasses), in accordance with the riches and the generosity of His gracious favor,

⁸Which He lavished upon us in every kind of wisdom and understanding (practical insight and prudence)

► The purpose of this writing is because God wants you to know that where He has planned to take you, none of the baggage of your flesh or your natural life can go! He wants and needs you to be free and clear in your mind and in Him. He already accepts you, approves of you, and has chosen you. Surrender the outcome of your life to Him, and He will deal with the ugly stuff.

Say out loud:

I am Perfect, and my Perfection is in Christ!

You are the container in which the light is carried and shines through. You are the light at the end of someone's dark tunnel. You are it. Stand up and shine!

CHAPTER 5

Power, Presence & Femininity

"Full of the power and the presence of His deity that's delivered through the function of my femininity."

Woman to Woman, behold the face of yourself in the face of your sister,
    the weakness you see in her is a call to show forth unafraid love.

Woman to Woman, behold the face of yourself in eyes that are crying for a love that is lost, unreturned, or burned, and show forth the strength of compassion to heal.

Woman to Woman, behold the face of your daughter through the uncertain eyes of your youth and remember that wisdom still needs time to grow as it is still growing in you.

Woman to Woman, Sister to Sister, the love you seek will be found in the need you meet,
    in the truth you embrace and the lies you finally release, in the pain you set free, in the fears you reject
    and in the embracing of an uncertain future, you'll soon learn to respect.

PERFECTION

Woman to Woman, don't fall in love with you, fall in love with the fact that you were thought of and became a finished idea by a creator greater than you and made to be an extension of the love that flows from woman to woman to woman to… Woman to Woman is the embodiment of life that never dies. You are Woman.

—J. Wright Middleton

Have you ever made the statements?
"I don't get along with other women."
"I don't like women. I get along better with men."

If you have, then your insecurity is speaking, and it's time for you to confront it face to face. Pride will say to you right now, "I'm not insecure!" and if pride is true, then how can you not get along with what you are? Think about it. You are the very thing that you claim you don't get along with. It's a form of self-hatred.

If you cannot celebrate another woman, encourage another woman, help build up, lift up and inspire another woman without feeling like you're losing something yourself, then insecurity has set up residence in you.

One of the main keys to being secure with who you are is recognizing that your sister's strengths do not take away from you or lessen your presence. Knowing who you are, and being comfortable in your own skin, empowers you to give to others and not feel like anything is being taken away from you.

We say things like, "Women are too catty, too petty, jealous, don't trust them around your man." If that is the assessment you have about the same thing you are, then is it fair to say that you might be capable or guilty of those same attributes? I want us to be clear - when you judge others, you may be guilty of doing the same (paraphrased: Matthew 7).

The statement, "I don't get along with women," is also a defense mechanism to keep you from feeling like you have to compete with other women. It's an armor that's worn to self-protect from perceived judgment. It's the voice that points out everything you're not, in comparison to someone else. When in reality, you don't have to compare yourself to anyone.

A woman in a room full of men has no competition, but instead, she lavishes on the idea of possibly being the desire of someone's or everyone's affection. My godmother made a very insightful statement to me; she said, *"The nature of a man is to lust after a woman. The nature of a woman is to be lusted after."*

We (women) use a variety of coping mechanisms to cover up insecurity. Anything that brings us attention, praise, or approval will suffice as an adequate tool, i.e., relationships, expensive clothing, money, dressing provocatively, education, multiple sexual partners, a bad attitude, success, etc., And anything that challenges or threatens us in receiving that praise, attention or approval becomes an enemy. I know this may be hard to swallow, but it is true. Think about it.

Do a little exercise and answer this question.

When was the first time you felt like you weren't good enough or felt like you had to compete for attention and affection? Was it when a boyfriend left you to be with someone else? Was it when your dad left your mom and started another family with another woman, and that woman's daughter received the attention you didn't? Maybe it was in school and the boy you liked, liked you and someone else. You waited anxiously to find out which one he liked more or which one he would pick knowing that if he didn't pick you everyone would talk about it. The day comes and you find out he picked the other girl. This is the day you start to believe that women are your competition and you will forever be in a game of comparison.

If you can identify that event, you will have found the date that insecurity walked in your front door and set up residence, and if you fully acknowledge it, you will be empowered to escort insecurity right out the same door.

Am I saying that we will have kumbaya moments with every woman we meet? No. But we definitely should never participate in dismissing our sisters based on our own weaknesses and fears. Insecurity will rob you of your femininity and your strength to empower your sister.

Your power, presence, and femininity are gifts to you from your creator. They are to be used to lift up, inspire, motivate and comfort. When a woman knows who she is and sees herself through the love and grace of God, she can't help but reflect that to others. She doesn't want to see her sisters beneath her or less than her because, truth-be-told we all come from the same cloth, and we all need the same savior.

Your presence should make others feel safe. Your power should make others feel like they are worthy, and your femininity should make everything look beautiful and make everyone around you feel beautiful.

"THEY HAVE ENEMIES"
fear, anger, rejection

There are enemies that will come against your power, presence, and femininity. We've already discussed one; the others are fear, anger, and rejection.

Fear, Anger & Rejection will sabotage your greatness.

I know what it's like to feel unsure, insecure, and inferior. I've been friends with low self-esteem, feelings of invisibility and inadequacy, and all the while knowing that God has put something special and unique in me like He has done in all of us. Yet my uncertainty and lack of direction overshadowed that little voice that was saying, "You are special."

The combination of displaced greatness and fear was tormenting. I knew I could do anything, but I was too afraid to try. I was afraid of failure, afraid to set goals for fear of not meeting the goals. I was playing a very difficult mental acrobatic game between liberty and perceived liberty. I was free in front of people and internally chained, and the time came when I had to confront my own chaos. The only way liberty would have its way was if I participated with the Holy Spirit.

My first call to action was when my husband went on a business trip to Los Angeles. There had been a car service to take him to the airport, and it would bring him home from the airport when he returned. I was home alone with the children and was quite peaceful. The first night everything was normal, and it was life as usual. The second night I had this urge to write down a few goals that I wanted to accomplish. I had done this before without recourse, but that night it was different.

I started with my first goal, which was to lose five pounds in ten days, but I stopped in fear before I could finish writing. Fear of once again creating a goal that I would not reach. This fear paralyzed me, and I just stared at the paper for a while because writing it down this time made me feel like I was committing to something that I may not be able to deliver.

My next thought was to explore this and see what fear was really doing to my life. I mean, if I couldn't write down that I wanted to lose five pounds, what in the world was really going on? So, I took a deep breath, said ok, and honestly faced myself by writing down everything that made me fearful.

As I began to write, that's when I realized how much fear ruled my life. It dawned on me that my fears had fears, and as I kept writing, the more ridiculous I felt. I was afraid of confrontation for fear there would be an argument and I would be rejected. I was afraid to set a mark that I would not reach and be deemed, in my eyes, a failure. I placed another gold star on the ever-growing list of things I started and never finished. My past experiences dictated my present, and fear played a major role.

After making my list, I prayed and told God I didn't want to be afraid anymore. Little did I know that my deliverance from fear would require my active participation.

You see, in Christianity, sometimes it's presented as though if we pray hard enough, things will just miraculously change. Occasionally that may be true, but the majority of the time, it's not. In your deliverance, you must be ever-present, alive, and active, just like the Word of God, and trust that God is serious when He says He is perfecting everything that concerns you.

PERFECTION

The night before my husband came home, he called me to inform me that I would have to pick him up from the airport. I internally panicked because I was afraid to drive on the highway, but I calmly replied, "how do I get there?" He told me and asked me if I was going to be okay, I told him yes, and we said goodnight.

The next morning when I awoke, everything was quiet and still. It felt like the earth stopped moving, and I felt like a little child getting ready to climb a big mountain. Nonetheless, I got in the car and headed to I495. When I got on the highway, I remembered my husband saying to stay in the middle lane all the way to Philadelphia International Airport. I think there is no protection in the middle lane, but I'll follow his instruction anyway.

As I'm driving, I'm looking at all the other cars speeding past me, and I'm tempted to go above the speed limit because I don't want to look like I don't know what I'm doing. It was then that the Holy Spirit began to speak to me. He said, *"Don't look at those other cars. Just stay in your lane. Your purpose is to get to the destination safely, not quickly. These cars are moving fast because they are familiar with this road; you're not. Just drive your lane and keep your eyes in front of you. Run your race."*

See, the goal wasn't for me to get there quickly; the goal was for me to get there confidently and safely. To be fully dependent on His ability to care for me, protect me, and grow me. As long as I drove with the focus of trying to keep up with what was going on around me, tragedy would have been inevitable. I would have been driving through someone else's experience, someone else's windshield (vision), or someone else's rearview mirror (past). How many of us try to live our lives through another's expectations?

Needless to say, I settled down, took a deep breath, and repeated what the Holy Spirit said all the way to the airport, and I made it there safely. I was so excited when I arrived because I had conquered my fear of driving on the highway. I did what He said, and it worked out for my good and for the benefit of another.

I did it! I did it by facing it on God's terms, God's way, and in God's time. And I learned that His time is whenever I'm ready. If you're waiting on God—stop—because He's really waiting on you.

God has spoken to me over the years and given me numerous words of direction, encouragement, and commands. He has taught me how to hear His voice as well as the voice of the enemy in times when the two can seem like they are intertwined. He's shown me how to fight in the spirit when my flesh was crying out for action. He's wooed me, pursued, corrected, and loved me unconditionally.

Whenever I've reached a place of having to put my faith in action, at every interval, I've usually put one foot in the water and kept the other in the boat, and when the boat began to drift, causing my feet to spread further and further apart, I'd jump back in the boat. I'd pull my foot that was in the water out and stay in a place that seemed to be producing safety, but it wasn't safe; it was restraint.

I was choosing to remain a slave in Egypt or even a wanderer in the desert but not to go and possess what God had waiting for me. Because I was afraid of the cost, I was afraid of the pain, I was afraid of failure, and I didn't want to fight. So, the enemy beat me up every chance I gave him.

When I saw others confidently operating in their gifts, I judged it as arrogance and pride. I shied away from those that spoke with boldness and surety about what they were doing and who they were for fear that they would see the holes that lived inside of me.

I surrounded myself with people that were just as or even more damaged than I was because it made me look and sound like I had it all together. I looked like I had no sicknesses, so I needed no physician. Not me; my cancer was a private affair, as pride would make me believe. It was invisible to those weaker than I was, and it ran from those stronger than I could ever hope to be.

Total bondage is what I allowed to become my normal function. So today, ladies, hear me as I implore you, encourage you, motivate you, and command you to stand up, be counted, and embrace the life that God intended for you to have.

Don't be like the man who stayed at the poolside for 38 years, waiting for someone else to put him in the healing waters. Because when you stay there too long, your excuses become your crutch, and they facilitate your sickness and cause you to continually stay in a place of complacency and failure.

Live the life that God has given you to the fullest. Lay aside every weight, sin, laziness, fear, and doubt that easily beset you and give way to the wind and the spirit of God that is speaking to you, calling you and moving you to progress and completion.

"ANGER"

There comes a time when you have to face the fight between your soul and your spirit. As women, we have to admit that there are instances when our emotions are not being harnessed with the

Word of God, and we respond to the situations of life with lifeless, non-regenerated weaponry. If someone makes you angry, you want to "tell them off." If someone hurts you, revenge becomes an option. God has positioned you to live a higher and fuller life. You are a woman of poise, dignity, honor, and elegance.

When we take the tactics of our old nature and hold them like they are secret weapons we are allowing our flesh to take pleasure in the freedom of being able to act out in any form or fashion, and then we look for a pat on the back to approve or validate our ungodly and inhumane acts.

Anger displaced is a weakening emotion. The amount of energy used to carry anger is emotionally and mentally depleting. When we do not use anger to bring change it turns into acts of aggression. Anger displaced is used to teach consequential lessons, to intimidate or control. Anger displaced can be used to bring harm to others instead of bringing change to ourselves. Remember that you are God's child, and you live for an audience of one.

Today, you are being beckoned to look at what's natural and what's spiritual and actively apply God's word to your life. How do you do that? When you want to hate, choose to love. When you want to complain, choose to pray. When you want to yell (or cuss), choose to listen. When you want to give control of your life to someone else just to keep the peace, **don't**, and ask for strength. It will come. It did for me. I am not, by any stretch of the imagination, suggesting that this is easy, because it is not; but I am offering another perspective that is obtainable. Learn to believe and act upon God's word with tears streaming down your cheeks and a lump in your throat if necessary. The only way you'll overcome what hinders you is when you are at the moment of testing, and you choose to do what

PERFECTION

will help you pass the test instead of giving up and accepting the failure. Draw your line in the sand and choose not to cross it. Set your own inner boundaries. Life and death are in front of you; which one will you choose?

A woman ruled by love and grace is a woman of strength. A woman moved by purpose is a Proverbs 31 woman. A woman able to learn a lesson from every challenge and resolve within herself not to be average in any area is a woman of excellence.

Proverbs 31 Commentary:

Proverbs has a lot to say about women. How fitting that the book ends with a picture of a woman of strong character, great wisdom, many skills, and great compassion. Some people have the mistaken idea the ideal woman in the bible is retiring, servile, and entirely domestic. Not so! This woman is an excellent wife and mother. She is also a manufacturer, importer, manager, realtor, farmer, seamstress, upholsterer, and merchant. Her strength and dignity do not come from her amazing achievements, however. They are a result of her reverence for God. In our society, where appearance counts for so much, it may surprise you that her appearance is never mentioned. Her attractiveness comes entirely from her character.

The woman described in this chapter has outstanding abilities. Her family's social position is high. In fact, she may not be one woman at all-she may be a composite portrait of ideal womanhood.

Do not see her as a model to imitate in every detail. See her instead as an inspiration to be all you can be. We can't be just like her, but we can learn from her industry, integrity, and resourcefulness.

—Tyndale Life Application Bible NLT

Believe that God is with you, and if He is for you, He's more than the world and anyone that can be against you. Besides, who can stand against the almighty God? He's the creator of this heaven and this earth. He's also the creator of the new heaven and the new earth. Put your confidence in Him and allow Him to set your mind at ease. He will cause all that He has ordained for your life to manifest. He will complete the good work that He started in you. He will be your refuge, your helper, and your protector. He will guide the steps that you take.

All of this may sound like an insurmountable feat or a huge amount of hype, but it is not. Changing the way you think and what you believe is paramount in being able to walk in your power, establishing your presence, and embracing your femininity.
Your place and position is not to fear but to transition, break free & fly. Your presence is awaited. Your power is established. Your femininity is an expression of God.

"REJECTION"

What if they don't like me?
What if I look foolish?
What if he walks out?

Past experiences of abandonment or possibly embarrassment can cause the fear of being rejected. We can begin questioning our value, wondering if we are good enough and think we have to prove our worthiness. Feeling rejected stings and to prevent the "feeling" we will do everything we can to control all circumstances and outcomes. Fighting tooth and nail to prove we are right. Unable to accept if we've made a mistake because being wrong means, (to the person that fears rejection), you are wrong as a human being. Sometimes we'll even try to beat others to the punch and reject ourselves by maintaining low self-esteem and expressing self-depreciation. It's exhausting. But God is so kind that He has rescued us from all of it - especially ourselves.

When rejection has been reinforced at different stages of life it's easy to think it's part of your DNA, forgetting that certain types of denial are just a part of life. For instance, not getting the job, being passed up for a promotion, or the guy you like doesn't share the same affection. These are all things that come with living but they do not define your worth or your place in the world.

There is no perfection, only life.

Milan Kundera

CHAPTER 6

Reflection

"He thought it was not robbery to become like me, so certainly I must be the best me you'll ever see."

I remember the day I gave my life to Christ. The preacher, a woman, extended the gift of salvation, and I began to feel butterflies in my belly. I knew I had come to church that Sunday determined to answer the call, so I didn't expect to be nervous. But I was; however, my determination was stronger. I rose to my feet and walked down a short aisle that felt like 3 miles at the time. The preacher said, "Do you want to accept Jesus Christ into your heart?" I said, "I do, but I feel like I need to do something." She responded, "What are you going to do?

You can't buy Him anything, and you can't take Him out for dinner; all you have to do is accept what he did on the cross and the blood He shed for you." I said okay, still not sure, I closed my eyes and repeated a prayer that I can't remember anymore, and that was it. When I opened my eyes, I was different. Everything was different. I had a miraculous conversion. My heart was sold out, and Jesus was now my Lord and Savior. I instantly stopped getting drunk, smoking weed, cussing, and being angry. I spent time in prayer, always talking to the Lord. He began to give me dreams that would show me things happening or things to come. I saw my prayers being answered quickly, and there were times that I could tangibly feel His presence.

After such a dynamic experience, you would think that I would undoubtedly know who God was and who I was in Him; regrettably,

I did not. My early experiences were the proof He gave me to let me know that He's real, but now I had to get to know His character and learn to trust Him. I had to discover who He was beyond theory and recognize who He was in me. He and I were becoming one.

I went through many years of misconception and believing lies about how God loved me and what would keep Him loving me. I always thought and was told many times that my emotions, the way I felt, didn't mean anything to God. So to gain approval from my heavenly father, I endured and submitted myself to harsh treatment so He would accept me. I obeyed Him in the way I thought would render me kindness, love, acceptance, and joy from Him. Scriptures became the chains of bondage instead of the pathway to life and receiving love that I didn't have to work for. I didn't understand what it meant to have perfect love living in and loving on me.

Have you ever had that kind of love? I mean a love you didn't have to do anything to obtain. Think about that for a moment. Has there ever been anyone in your life (that you can remember) who totally accepted and loved you, someone that gave you "free love?" The kind of love you can test with your rebellion, and it never goes away?

"IS THAT WHERE IT CAME FROM?"

If you grew up in a healthy relationship with a father, step or biological, then you would understand the concept of "free love." It's love that comes without any requirements or demands. It's the love you receive from your parents just because you were born. They want to protect you because it hurts them to see you in pain. They want to provide for you because they don't want to see you go without; the love that sacrifices itself for you.

If you've grown up without that experience and the only male relationships you've ever had were romantic ones, then this concept might be difficult for you to grasp. Consequently, romantic relationships are transactional. They come with clauses, requirements, and prerequisites. Romantic relationships require your participation and are not there for your pleasure alone. Sometimes they can be one decision away from being non-existent, or they can be completely healing. But their permanency is conditional.

However, there will come a day when you will wonder if the person you're with will love you regardless of what you do or don't do. I know it sounds off the wall, but it is acutely definite. You'll begin to crave the love that will be there even if you reject the one offering it.

You'll find yourself testing the emotional strength of your significant other. Shelling out argumentative conversations and wanting him/her to accept it, understand it and not get upset about it. You want that significant other to love you no matter what. You want to test the durability of their love. You want to see and hear the sacrifice that's being made. How do I know?

My husband and I have a blended family. When we married, I had a young son, and he had two children. I instantly fell in love with them. They were great kids.

However, there was an occasion when we were shopping for his daughter, and the amount that he wanted to spend on sneakers was more than I thought he should. It wasn't a special occasion. There was just no reason I could see why he would spend this large amount of money on a pair of sneakers. I mean, this type of expenditure, to me, should be the result of a good deed or extraordinary school performance. I was very uncomfortable. Nevertheless, we bought the sneakers. On another occasion, I watched how tenderly and lovingly he treated his daughter. How he wanted to serve her and do whatever she needed at the time.

In watching this, I found myself getting uncomfortable again. I was actually feeling jealous. The thought of this jealousy going on inside of me was shocking and embarrassing. How could I, a grown woman, be jealous of an 11-year-old little girl with her father?

I mulled this over for the rest of the day. I was totally disturbed by the circumstances surrounding what I was feeling more than the feeling itself because I knew I loved this little girl. I asked God about it, and He willingly and quickly answered.

The love I was witnessing between my husband and his daughter was something I had never experienced. I was 23 years old and had never experienced love that didn't require an act on my part. The truth is I wanted my husband to love me without my participation. I wanted to be rewarded for doing nothing special. I wanted gifts and non-sexual affection. I wanted him to love me like a father. I wanted what I didn't have as a child, and I didn't even know I was missing it until I saw it displayed between my husband and his daughter.

Now that I know, what can I do? Do I pressure my husband to treat me like a daughter and make him responsible for my wholeness? I couldn't expect my husband to love me like a father. I didn't know where my biological or stepfather lived, and if I did, what good would it do? There was no answer or insight to help me experience what I had been missing all those years. There was no one capable of filling this void…except Christ.

God let me know that He is the only one that is fully capable of loving me in that way. He was the answer to my empty space. It was Him that loved me while I was rejecting Him. He died for me when I didn't even know His name. His love never changed. His love redeemed me. His love continues when others are unable to go on. His love came without conditions and didn't require extra special performances. He loves me because I am His.

This revelation of my Father's love for me shed light in my life. I wanted someone to love me when I was wrong, when I acted ugly and when I felt weak. I wanted a love that wanted to love me even though that love saw all of my shortcomings. I wanted a father who thought everything I did was wonderful, and if I gave him a simple hug, that would be enough.

When I realized what I needed, I cried out to my Heavenly Father, and He answered my cry. He reminded me, as often as I needed, that He loved me and His love was unwavering. He would fight for me. He would stand up for me. His banner (announcement) over me is love. He told me He would always be my helper, and He would never leave me. The love he poured out on me filled my holes and healed my soul. It gave me the confidence to stand, knowing that my daddy had my back.

I began to rehearse the love God had for me. He told me He chose me when I felt overlooked and second place. He sent people to give me gifts and words of encouragement when I felt unappreciated. He told me I was the crowning of His glory when I had no clue what my life meant. He told me that He created me as a tri-part being of spirit, soul, and body and that every part of me mattered.

My emotions and how I felt mattered to Him, and they had a place in a Christian's life.

He reminded me that the first time I heard His voice was when I didn't believe Him or accept Him. I found my mind and my gifts through communication and communion with Him. He told me He could be touched by the feeling of my pain. He told me I was created for love. He told me He was the love.

The light that shines from within comes from what we believe. You have to believe that you are here for a purpose and on purpose. You have to believe that you are vital to the movement of life on earth. You have to believe that your flavor is the missing ingredient when you are invited to the party.

There is no real beauty without some imperfections.

James Salter

CHAPTER 7

Validation & Acceptance

"I know who I am & I like who I be. Spiritual, Intellectual, Beautiful & Free. I accept me."

After my mother died, and maybe even before then, there was a time when my life was not my own. I would morph into whatever someone else wanted, needed, or threw away. I had no clear vision of myself. It was as if I would look at myself in a mirror, and when I walked away, I forgot what I looked like. I wasn't able to set up boundaries because I didn't know how and the only guide I had for what I wouldn't do, was my pride. I was a parentless teenager with my emotions as my compass. And my emotions said, do what you want, when you want; so I did.

Synonyms for validation:

Confirmation, acceptance, affirmation, authorization, corroboration, endorsement, proof, recognition, verification, accord, admission, agreement, approval, assent, authentication, consent, evidence, nod, okay, passage, passing, sanction, substantiation, support, witness, accepting, affirming, authenticating, authorizing, corroborating, go ahead, stamp of approval, verifying

Antonyms for validation:

Denial, disagreement, disapproval, dissension, opposition, refusal, rejection, veto.

I started this chapter with definitions because I wanted you to be sure about the meaning of the word "validation."

After becoming a born-again believer and getting married, I went through a series of devastating events. I was broken. I took the victim's posture and accepted everything thrown at me. I felt hopeless and helpless and kept holding on to one bad experience after the other.

It would take many encounters with the Holy Spirit and the desire for freedom to open me to the truth. He gave me a scripture that changed my life and began my journey of freedom and wholeness.

Knowing the truth really makes you free. But it is also the truth you accept and the truth you tell that leads to inner freedom.

"VALIDATION"

> ***Romans 6:16***—*"Do you know that to whom you present yourselves, slaves, to obey, you are that one's slaves whom you obey, whether of sin leading to death or of obedience leading to righteousness"?*

This means that whatever or whomever you willingly submit to, you give them power over you—to lead you to life or death. When I read that, I said, "WHAT!!!???, What in the world…How did this happen…I was a punk?!" (LOL)

When you willingly give someone power over you, they have the authority and right to drag you wherever they want because you have given them permission. Someone could be leading you through their own insecurity, control issues, or fears.

When you identify what or whom you have given control of your life to—take it back. Your *creator* is the only one with the right and the ability to have control of your life, and the fabulous thing is that He gives that control to you.

> **Galatians 5:1**—*Stand fast therefore in the liberty by which Christ has made us free and be not entangled again with a yoke of bondage.*

The realization of these scriptures is what started the journey of perfection. The poem was born out of me beginning to allow God to validate me and allowing myself to agree with what He said—about me.

> **Hebrews 4:12**—*For the word of God is quick, and powerful, and sharper than any two-edged sword, piercing even to the dividing asunder of soul and spirit, and of the joints and marrow, and is a discerner of the thoughts and intents of the heart. (KJV)*

PERFECTION

God means what he says. His powerful Word is sharp as a surgeon's scalpel, cutting through everything, whether doubt or defense, laying us open to listen and obey. Nothing and no one is impervious to God's Word. We can't get away from it—no matter what. (*Msg.*)

God has made us to function in every environment He has created. He created us soul, body, and spirit. There isn't any part of our personality or individuality that surprises Him. He is interested in every area of our lives.

He made nature for our eyes, ears, noses, and hands to enjoy. He's given man the ability to seek out knowledge and create things for the occupation of his brain and his intellect. He's given us bodies that can reproduce, heal themselves if treated properly, and carry us on this earth. Our bodies and physical senses are what respond to our creations in the world. Our souls discern the information that the earth transmits, and we respond accordingly with our emotions. Our spirits are connected to Him through Christ by the Holy Spirit in order that we may submit every one of these other areas of our being to His guidance. It's in Him that we should live, move and have our being.

He's sent His son to redeem us from the wages of sin so we can live with Him eternally. You can live a spiritual life and have natural enjoyment. God has given us all things to enjoy, and He's given us all things that pertain to life and godliness. We all have different preferences due to the variations that God created. One may like green, and another may like blue, yet both are God's creations.

Love who you are. Your uniqueness comes from God, and He wants your expression of Him to be seen on the earth.

When I first started to write poetry, I only wrote it for myself as a release for my anger. I never intended for anyone to read my poems or for me to be found reading them in front of others. The more I wrote, the more I became comfortable with the process of writing. Then one night, I discovered Def Poetry Jam, a 90's comedy television show. I heard poets speaking and performing like I had never heard before. Up until that point, I looked at Maya Angelou and Nikki Giovanni, who were reciting and reading their poetry with powerful poise and intellectual flair. But this new breed of poet had a flavor that appealed to the younger masses. I would watch and wonder and say to myself, "I can't do it like that."

I watched them perform for a few years, and every time I watched, I would say to myself, "I can't do it like that. I don't have that kind of rhythm." After a long while, my husband would say to me, "you don't have to do it like them. You have your own flow." And even though he was saying it, I kept hearing— "I can't do it like that."

Then one day, it dawned on me that the people I truly admired didn't do it like that either. They each had their own "flow," and they were wonderful, well-respected, and renowned poets. It was then that I understood it was okay for me to have my own style; as long as I am confident in it, everyone will have to respect it. I began to accept my gift and its presentation, and I love it. I do what I was given to do, and I do it my way. And it's okay. You, dear beloved, should do what you were given to do with your own stamp on it. The approval you want and are seeking was given to you when you were created. God has given you something that you do well, extraordinarily even, and let that be enough to give you the confidence you need.

If there was a formula that gave people the awareness of their God-given awesomeness, it would be:

> Acceptance + Faith x God = A Bold, Beautiful, Unstoppable, Perfect, Creative You! **In Christ, you are made complete and perfect. (Colossians 2:10)**

Beautifully Human

God, you've made me beautifully and wonderfully human. You've placed yourself in me to allow me to connect to your deity... so that I wouldn't be forever lost

God, you've made me wonderfully and beautifully human. I am the design of your mind captured in your image...so that I wouldn't be forever lost

God, you've made me beautifully and wonderfully human. You've breathed the breath, your breath, your life, in me...and **I** *became a living soul.*

You continue to allow me to be the earthly expression of your heavenly spirit. My love—is your love. My life—is your life. Mines—is yours.

"Perfection Is Not What You Do, It's Who You Are."

How do you improve something you didn't create and don't have the blueprint for its existence? The perfection that this book is built upon is not established by any means of human capability. This chapter is short because trying to explain "perfection" would make me repeat what is already written. So instead, I'll just let you read it for yourself.

- I am not the great "I am," but by the grace of God, I am what I am. *(Exodus 3:14, John 8: 24,28,58, 1 Corinthians 15:10).*
- I am the salt of the earth and the light of the world. *(Matthew 5:13-14).*
- I am Christ's friend. I am chosen and appointed by Christ to bear His fruit. *(John 1:12; 15:15-16).*
- I am a son of God; God is spiritually my Father. *(Romans 8:14-15, Galatians 3:26; 4:6).*
- I am loved. *1 John 3:3.*
- I am accepted. *Ephesians 1:6.*
- I am a child of God. *John 1:12.*
- *I am Jesus' friend. John 15:14.*
- *I am a joint heir with Jesus, sharing His inheritance with Him. Romans 8:17.*

PERFECTION

- *I am united with God and one spirit with Him. 1 Corinthians 6:17.*
- *I am a temple of God. His Spirit and His life lives in me. 1 Corinthians 6:19.*
- *I am a member of Christ's body. 1 Corinthians 12:27.*
- *I am a Saint. Ephesians 1:1.*
- *I am redeemed and forgiven. Colossians 1:14.*
- *I am complete in Jesus Christ. Colossians 2:10.*
- *I am free from condemnation. Romans 8:1.*
- *I am a new creation because I am in Christ. 2 Corinthians 5:17.*
- *I am chosen by God, holy and dearly loved. Colossians 3:12.*
- *I am established, anointed, and sealed by God.*
- *2 Corinthians 1:21.*
- *I do not have a spirit of fear, but of love, power, and a sound mind. 2 Timothy 1:7.*
- *I am God's co-worker. 2 Corinthians 6:1.*
- *I am seated in heavenly places with Christ. Eph. 2:6.*
- *I have direct access to God. Ephesians 2:18.*
- *I am chosen to bear fruit. John. 15:16.*
- *I am one of God's living stones, being built up in Christ as a spiritual house. 1 Peter 2:5.*
- *I have been given exceedingly great and precious 2 Peter 1:4.*
- *I can always know the presence of God because He never leaves me. Hebrews. 13:5.*
- *God works in me to help me do the things He wants me to do. Philippians 2:13.*
- *I can ask God for wisdom, and He will give me what I need. James 1:5.*

If you are looking for any other explanation of perfection, you are looking through the wrong eyes. Our flesh will always look for a way to excel above another. It always wants to have the upper hand on someone. But the reality is no matter where we are from, what we have or don't have, we all need the same blood from the same Savior. In God's eyes, we're all the same, starting from the same deficit, and He is the only one who has the way out.

Welcome to Perfection.

EPILOGUE

How blessed is God! And what a blessing he is! He's the Father of our Master, Jesus Christ, and takes us to the high places of blessing in him. Long before he laid down earth's foundations, he had us in mind, had settled on us as the focus of his love, to be made whole and holy by his love. Long, long ago, he decided to adopt us into his family through Jesus Christ. (What pleasure he took in planning this!) He wanted us to enter into the celebration of his lavish gift-giving by the hand of his beloved Son.

Because of the sacrifice of the Messiah, his blood poured out on the altar of the cross. We're a free people—free of penalties and punishments chalked up by all our misdeeds. And not just barely free, either. *Abundantly* free!

He thought of everything, provided for everything we could possibly need, letting us in on the plans he took such delight in making. He set it all out before us in Christ, a long-range plan in which everything would be brought together and summed up in him, everything in deepest heaven, everything on planet earth. It's in Christ that we find out who we are and what we are living for. Long before we first heard of Christ and got our hopes up, he had his eye on us and designed us for glorious living; part of the overall purpose he is working out in everything and everyone.

It's in Christ that you, once you heard the truth and believed it (this Message of your salvation), found yourselves home, free, signed, sealed, and delivered by the Holy Spirit. This signet from God is the first installment of what's coming, a reminder that we'll get everything God has planned for us, a praising and glorious life.

That's why, when I heard of the solid trust you have in the Master Jesus and your outpouring of love to all the followers of Jesus,

PERFECTION

I couldn't stop thanking God for you—every time I prayed, I'd think of you and give thanks. But I do more than thank you. I ask the God of our Master, Jesus Christ, the God of glory—to make you intelligent and discerning in knowing him personally, your eyes focused and clear, so that you can see exactly what it is he is calling you to do, grasp the immensity of this glorious way of life he has for his followers, oh, the utter extravagance of his work in us who trust him—endless energy, boundless strength!

All these energy issues from Christ: God raised him from death and set him on a throne in deep heaven, in charge of running the universe, everything from galaxies to governments, with no name and no power exempt from his rule. And not just for the time being, but *forever*. He is in charge of it all, has the final word on everything and at the center of all this, Christ rules the church.

The church, you see, is not peripheral to the world; the world is peripheral to the church. The church is Christ's body, in which he speaks and acts, by which he fills everything with his presence. *Ephesians Chapter 1 Message Bible*

Ending with the perspective that all things come from Christ and in Him all things consist is a very sobering thought. And if perception is a reality which in turn, governs our perspective, let's make sure that one thing is the origin of our perception. The perfection of Christ is the perfection we live in.

Perfect love casts out all fear.

1 John 4:18

BONUS CHAPTER

Christ made us Perfect in God's eyes.

Hebrews 10:14

12 RULES OF PERFECTION

It's All About Perspective

These 12 rules are lessons that I've learned and discovered on my perfection journey. They helped me accept myself and others a little easier and a little more. They also took the edge off trying to prove myself. Number 1 is my favorite!

My 12 Rules of Perfection

1. **The key to always being right is to know when you're wrong.**

    It takes a true heart of humility to admit when you are wrong and to be able to take instruction. If you can admit that you miss it sometimes and you don't know everything, when you make a mistake, it won't hit you in the gut so hard. Being able to say, "I was wrong," will keep me from the temptation of being performance perfect.

2. **Perfection is not what you do; it's who you are.**

    The only thing that allows us to claim the perfection status is the fact that through the blood of Jesus Christ, we have been made perfect. So that when God sees us, He sees us without blame. That's it.

3. **Embrace your sphere of influence and don't envy another's.**

   Be grateful for the territory you have been given and rock it out until the lights go off, because you have what you need for where you are going.

4. **Be painfully honest with yourself.**

   Self-deception is the worst kind of deception. If you know your flaws, your strengths, your likes and dislikes, you will be able to stand your ground, walk with confidence (not arrogance) and shine like a diamond.

5. **Learn to distinguish between weeds and flowers.**

   In a garden, weeds can grow and bud flowers that from a distance look healthy and look like they belong. But when you get up close, you realize these disguised weeds are there to kill the real flowers and destroy the flower bed. So, find the weeds and get rid of them.

6. **Acknowledge your limitations and use someone else's strength.**

   Knowing what you can and cannot do is so freeing, because you don't put unnecessary expectations on yourself or others.

A body is made of many parts, and each part has its own specific function. Find your part and play it well.

7. **Doing your personal best is perfection.**

   Your personal best is applying your whole self to the task at hand and giving it all you have. And if it's still not right, go back to number 6 and find someone who can do it better. ☺

8. **Use mistakes as an opportunity to learn what not to do again and what to do better.**

   Insanity is doing the same thing over and over and expecting a different result. When you mess up, own it, look at it, find the hole and don't do it again.

9. **Own your choices. Take responsibility for your actions.**

   A person that refuses to take responsibility for their actions will always look to blame someone else and remain a victim of circumstances.

10. **Accept people for who they are.**

    Never try to make someone into who you want them to be; it sends a subliminal message that they are not good enough to be in your company.

11. **Think before you speak because your words are a direct reflection of what you believe in your heart.**

    Authenticity means being genuine. When you say what you believe and mean what you say, you will attract people who respect your honesty and free them to be genuine as well.

12. **Love the life you live and create a life you can love.**

    Hey, you only get one…you might as well live it the best way you can. God gave it to you.

Notes to My Perfect Self

Write your rules of perfection to help govern your continuous journey to the life you were created to live.

What do I like about Me?

What do I need from my relationships?

What am I afraid of not getting?

What are my strengths?

What is my personal mission statement?

What do I want to change about me?

What about me do I need to celebrate?

J. Wright Middleton

AUTHOR

SPEAKER

PLAYWRIGHT

TALK SHOW HOST

DIRECTOR

ENTREPRENEUR

Janelle is CEO/ Owner of a publishing service company (Vision Directives, LLC) and a multi-faceted lifestyle production company (JWM Productions). Our mission is to **Enlighten, Inspire, Transform and Entertain**. We are fully committed to producing books, TV shows, plays, workshops and podcasts that speak to various functions of human relationships.

We have currently produced plays, books, a self-esteem curriculum, and a mother/daughter workshop with panel discussion. We are also in partnership with a music production company, Big Herb's Music/BMI which is owned and run by Grammy-nominated producer Herb Middleton. The value of this connection has given JWM Productions access to a high caliber of artist and professionals from the entertainment industry.

Our agenda is to empower people to walk in wholeness and to be a full of expression of the gifts and talents God has given them.

J. Wright-Middleton

AVAILABLE CONTENT

J. Wright Middleton | www.jwrightmiddleton.com

***Like Mother, Like Daughter, Like* Me**-watch three generations journey through truth, love and forgiveness. A musical comedy that helps strengthen mother daughter relationships.

Sunday Brunch Marriage Uncovered-Four girlfriends from church get together to discuss their views on marriage; the desperate to be married, the never getting married, the "perfect marriage" and marriage through divorce. Dramatic Comedy.

The Magdalene Monologues-Real life testimonies of six women that have been touched by the delivering power of God. Dramatic Ministry.

  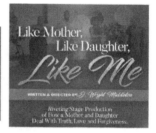

Made in the USA
Middletown, DE
06 March 2024

50907057R00060